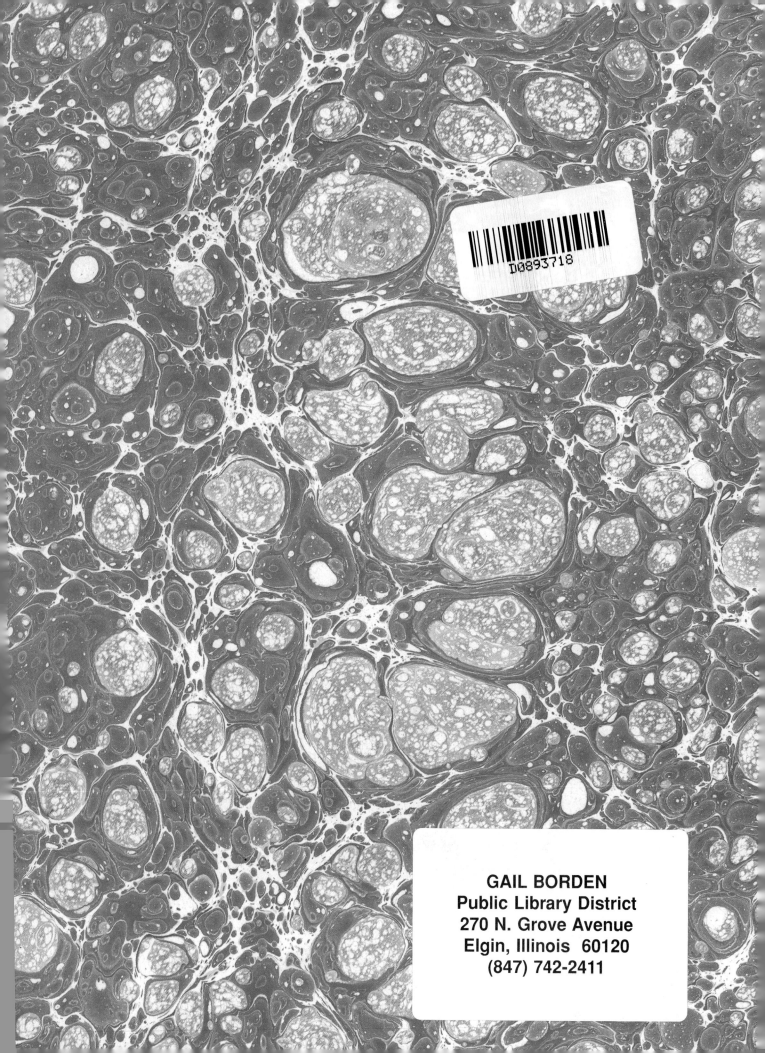

Saltbox *and* Cape Cod Houses

by Stanley Schuler

Revised & Expanded 2nd Edition

Schiffer Publishing Ltd®

4880 Lower Valley Road, Atglen, PA 19310 USA

Revised: 2000
Copyright © 1988 & 2000 by Stanley Schuler.
Library of Congess Catalog Card Number: 99-68638

ISBN: 0-7643-0998-6
Printed in China

Published by Schiffer Publishing Ltd.
4880 Lower Valley Road
Atglen, PA 19310
Phone: (610) 593-1777; Fax: (610) 593-2002
E-mail: Schifferbk@aol.com
Please visit our website catalog at **www.schifferbooks.com**

In Europe, Schiffer books are distributed by Bushwood Books
6 Marksbury Avenue Kew Gardens
Surrey TW9 4JF England
Phone: 44 (0)208-392-8585; Fax: 44 (0)208-392-9876
E-mail: Bushwd@aol.com

This book may be purchased from the publisher.
Include $3.95 for shipping. Please try your bookstore first.
We are interested in hearing from authors with book ideas on related subjects.
You may write for a free printed catalog.

Index to Houses

Contents

Past, Present and Future

In the arts the past returns again and again. This is particularly true in architecture. We may think that a certain architectural feature or practice is dead and gone forever, but of this nobody can be sure. Consider the Palladian window—just one of numerous possible examples. Andrea Palladio, the Italian renaissance architect, originated the Venetian Opening sometime before 1580. His followers developed it into the beautiful Palladian, or Venetian window, which was a common feature of great American and English homes until about 1800. Then architects and builders ignored it until just a few years ago. Today it is widely used in American houses.

Saltboxes and Cape Cod houses have enjoyed much the same experience. They came into being in the 1600s, thrived in the 1700s, disappeared from the new-home market almost completely in the 1800s, and have been resurrected in the 1900s. There are no statistics to gauge the popularity of American architectural styles, but it is my guess that the saltbox today is more popular than ever in the past and still gaining, and that, while the Cape has slipped a bit from its peak following World War II, it is still going strong. This is especially true in New England, where both styles started out. Elsewhere the inadequately named Contemporary house reigns supreme, but there are still a great many discerning people who prefer to reproduce the homes of our New England forebears.

What gives the saltbox and Cape their enduring qualities?

Capes and saltboxes developed from houses like those, left. The 1695 Cape (top) is on the King's Highway in Barnstable, Mass. The saltbox is the Deacon John Grave house, 1675, in Madison, Conn. The lean-to was added to the latter.

Their simplicity. Integrity. Practicality. And most of all, their unassuming charm.

A saltbox is a house with more than one story in front and only one full story in back. It has a peaked roof with an elongated rear slope, and the ridge is closer to the front of the house than to the back. It was called a saltbox because it is shaped like the wooden box in which our ancestors kept salt. In the South it is also known as a catslide house because cats presumably love to slide down the long roof on their bellies. (However, not all houses with catslide roofs are saltboxes; some one-story houses also have elongated rear roofs.)

Like most early architectural forms, the saltbox was not an American development even though it is much more prevalent here than abroad. The English put what they too called catslide roofs on homes long before Americans. Little Chesterford Farm, built circa 1320, and Priory Cottage in Bramber (15th century) have catslide roofs. In both cases, these were added to the original structures when extra living space was required within.

Saltboxes appeared in 17th century America for the same reason.

As soon as our earliest settlers felt established in New England, they started replacing the huts they had constructed right after they landed with permanent houses. Some of these were one-and-a-half stories tall; some were two. They were very small. Some of the two-story houses had four rooms—two up and two down on either side of a central chimney; others had only two rooms—one up and one down with the chimney at one end. When the owners of the two-room houses first needed more space, they built two matching rooms on the opposite side of the chimney (to which one or two new fireplaces were added). Then, when they needed to expand a second time, they built a lean-to across the back of the house. (The first expansion made by people who started out with four-room houses was also a lean-to.) The roof of the lean-to was made an extension of the existing rear roof slope. Usually it continued downward at the same angle as the old roof; occasionally it tilted upward very slightly like the take-off portion of a ski jump; but in either case it ended roughly seven feet above ground level so the occupants could enter the back door without stooping. Thus the first American saltboxes were born. The date was somewhere around 1650.

Roughly twenty-five years later, new houses were being built as saltboxes to start with. These are not always easy to distinguish from those with added lean-tos. At casual glance, there is nothing to tell you that the Lt. William Bushnell house on page 18 started life as a two-room, two-story house in 1680, was later expanded to a four-room house, and then acquired an added lean-to, while the Hoxie house (page 25) was built pretty much as is in 1675. Frequently, however, you may see a clear break between the original structure and the added lean-to. The break in the Hyland house (page 23), for instance, is at the end of the side overhangs; that in the Deacon John Grave house (page 4) is marked by a vertical board; that in the Capt. Thomas Newson house (page 36) is marked by a slight bend in the catslide roof.

The origins of the Cape are less clear. It probably evolved naturally and gradually from the crude one-room, one-and-a-half-story, steep-roofed houses with end

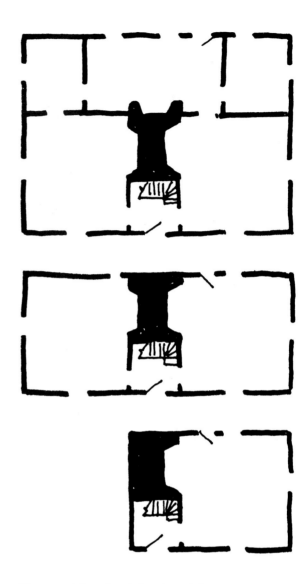

How a saltbox (top) developed from a two-story house with one room on ground floor (bottom).

chimneys that the Pilgrims had left in Europe and that they began to build about 1630 after they were certain their little colony would survive. But it is impossible to put a finger on a specific house and say, "This was the first true Cape." If the dates emblazoned on ancient houses today are accurate (some are, but many are not), the best claim to that title is held by the William Peck house in Old Lyme, Connecticut. It was ostensibly built in 1666—twelve years before the oldest known Cape still standing on Cape Cod. This raises the question: "How does it happen that the Cape Cod house is named after the Cape Cod peninsula if it did not originate there?" The answer is that no one in its early days thought to give it another name—in fact, they neglected to give it *any* name. Consequently, when the president of Yale at the start of the 19th century suggested that it be called the Cape Cod house, the name stuck. Furthermore, the William Peck house to the contrary, we cannot be certain that the Cape did not originate on Cape Cod.

But more important than this is what makes a Cape a Cape. Unlike a saltbox, easily defined and easily identified, the Cape Cod house does not lend itself to a simple, short definition.

In my earlier book *The Cape Cod House*, I described the Cape Cod house of the 17th and 18th centuries as follows:

It forms a compact rectangle. Even though additions are made later, the original structure usually stands out. It sits very close to the ground and generally faces south.

It has an unbroken gable roof, pitched steeply enough to provide living space with headroom underneath. The facade is approximately eight feet high. From sills to roof peak the house is approximately twenty feet high.

It has a massive chimney that rises through the roof ridge and is, in the largest Capes, centrally located between the gable ends.

It is of frame construction. The walls are clad with wood shingles or clapboards or both. The roof is wood-shingled. The rather small, multi-paned windows are placed close under the eaves.

The eaves and rakes project only a few inches beyond the walls.

There are as many as five windows of several sizes in the gables to light the upper floor. Exterior ornamentation is totally lacking.

The early Capes and saltboxes were built in three main sizes; however, the actual differences in size are more apparent in Capes than in saltboxes. Today they are called "full" houses, "three-quarter" houses and "half" houses.

The full house is by far the most common, although it may not have been so in early days. The front door is centered in the facade and is flanked on both sides by a pair of windows (but in some houses, especially in Connecticut, the door is flanked on both sides by a single window). The chimney is centered on the roof above the door. Full Capes were roughly 34 to 40 feet long and 28 feet wide. Full saltboxes were only slightly larger—36 to 42 feet long by 30 feet wide.

In the three-quarter house the door and chimney above it are somewhat off-center. There is one window on one side of the door and two windows on the other.

In the half house the front door and chimney are at one end of the house and there are two windows between the door and the other end of the house. Despite its location, the chimney was generally concealed within the house until it emerged through the roof. In Rhode Island, however, the back wall of the chimney sometimes served as the outside wall of the house (but it never projected beyond the house as chimneys in the southern colonies did). This kind of house is known as a stone-ender.

Capes were also built in other sizes, all of which are now quite rare. There were "quarter" houses, with only a single front window and door, and "double" houses, which were two full houses joined end to end. A third variant was the Cape Ann cottage, so named because it originated on Cape Ann, just north of Boston, and did not stray very far from there. It is simply a tiny Cape Cod house, usually with a gambrel roof.

Saltboxes and Cape Cod houses were also very much alike in other respects. In

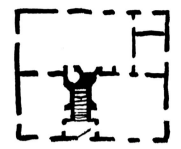

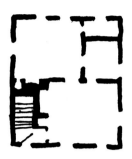

Full Cape   Three-quarter Cape   Half Cape

floor plan, for instance, saltboxes more or less mirrored the plans shown above for three different sizes of Cape. In both full and three-quarter houses, the front door opened into a cramped entry from which the stairs usually rose to the second floor; however, in saltboxes, the stairs customarily formed a shallow U because there was ample headroom for a person to stand upright at the top of the stairs, whereas he would have had to crawl on hands and knees if similar stairs were used in a Cape. There were two roughly square rooms, each with a fireplace, on either side of the entry. One, known as the parlor, was a fairly formal room though it often included a bed. The other was called the hall—a sort of all-purpose room for living, sleeping and occasional cooking. At the back of the house was the kitchen, or keeping room. It was long and rather narrow and had a very large fireplace and beehive oven. Depending on the family's requirements, there might be tiny rooms at one or both ends of the kitchen. One of these was likely to be the buttery, or pantry; the other one or two were bedrooms. In modern parlance, one of the bedrooms is known as the borning room because it was for new mothers and babies, but that name was not used in the past.

The second floor generally had two bedrooms, one on either side of the chimney. These may or may not have had small fireplaces. In addition, saltboxes had a long, narrow room behind the bedrooms. This was under the catslide roof and was lighted and ventilated by only single small windows at both ends; consequently the space was little better than an attic and was called the attic, although large families used it as a bunk room for children and servants. (Another smaller attic used for storage was on the third floor under the roof ridge.

In half houses, the room called the hall was eliminated on the first floor and one of the two bedrooms was eliminated on the second.

Both saltboxes and Capes were framed with great oak timbers held together by intricate wood joints and oak pegs. The principal members were the sills; the corner posts and the posts on either side of the front and back doors; the plates and girts laid across the tops of the posts to tie the four sides of the house together; and the huge summer beams—the largest timbers in the house—that bisected the house. These usually ran from the middle of the end girts to the middle of the chimney girts—that is, from one end of the house toward the other—but in some cases they ran from the front plate to the back plate at the middle of the parlor and hall.

The first-floor joists were mortised into the sills; the second floor and attic-floor joists, into the plates and summers.

The main roof supports were four very large rafters placed above the posts in the front and back walls. These were tied together by purlins running from gable end to gable end. There was no ridge board. Thick planks were laid vertically over this structure and shingles were applied on top.

The exterior walls of the houses were also sheathed with planks installed vertically between the sills and the horizontal timbers above. Shingles or clapboards covered them. Shingles were preferred for Capes, though some houses had clapboards on front and shingles elsewhere. Clapboards were favored for saltboxes.

In some of the earliest saltboxes the window sash were of the casement type and had small panes set in lead. But most houses—both saltboxes and Capes—had double-hung wood windows with wide muntins. The upper sash was fixed; only the lower sash slid up and down. To lock the latter against intruders, the home owner set a stout stick of wood diagonally between its top rail and one of the upper corners of the window frame. Current opinion to the contrary, exterior blinds were not used until the late 18th century; but an occasional house did have interior shutters.

Although our ancestors in the 17th century often displayed little interest in symmetry, they normally placed windows in the facades of their homes neatly. But the placement of windows on the sides and back of the house was likely to be eccentric. This was particularly true of the upper-story windows in Cape Cod houses. Henry Thoreau noted that the gable ends of Capes looked "as if each of the various occupants [of a house] had punched a hole [in the wall] where his necessities required it and according to his size and stature, without regard to outside effect." The closest thing to a standard arrangement consisted of two large windows in the middle of the gable flanked by two very small windows and a fifth very small window just below the roof peak.

Doorways were very simple. The doors at first were made of planks, but these were soon superseded by paneled doors. The door opening was cased with plain, flat boards. Across the top was a transom with four or five fixed lights. Later, as home owners grew interested in ornamenting their dwellings, Cape doorways were prettied up to some extent but they never were truly handsome because there was too little space for fine Georgian and Federal over-door treatment. Some 18th century saltboxes, however, had doorways of great beauty. In fact, one of the most beautiful and most often photographed entrances in the United States is to the Ashley house in Deerfield (Page 54).

Unlike the doorways, the fireplaces and chimneys of saltboxes and Capes were always beautiful. This was not because early New Englanders took pains to make them beautiful; they left the design and construction of gorgeous mantels and overmantels to the next generations. The beauty of the earliest fireplaces stemmed from their simplicity, their obvious practicality and their large to—in many kitchens—great size. Similarly, the beauty of the chimneys lay in their dimensions. They were not the pipe-stems that were often stuck on rooftops when stoves succeeded fireplaces as heat sources. And they were not the larger but still modest chimneys of today. They were sturdy, even massive, brick or sometimes stone structures that dominated the entire house. True, they dominated Capes more than saltboxes, because Capes are smaller and the rooftops are closer to the ground and therefore more visible. But make no mistake about it: the chimney of a saltbox is the crowning glory of that roof, too.

The roof, of course, is the principal point of difference between saltboxes and Capes and the full two-story Colonial homes that followed saltboxes.

The saltbox roof is unusual because of its extra-long rear slope which, if unbroken by dormers—as it was in ancient houses—usually rolls and waves and sags excessively as a result of the warpage of the rafters and purlins. It is also unusual because the front slope is shorter than the front roof slope of a Cape or conventional two-story Colonial. This is because the ridge is closer to the front wall than the ridge of a Cape or two-story house, and that in turn is because the ridge was originally centered on a house that was only one-room deep.

The top sketch illustrates the difference between the roofs of the three types of house. The heavy lines show the roofline of an actual saltbox—the Ogden house in Fairfield, Connecticut. The light lines represent a conventional two-story Colonial, and the broken line, a Cape. The latter two roofs are hypothetical but realistic. There is surprisingly little difference in the area of the three roofs (unless, of course, the lower part of a saltbox roof does not extend across the entire length of the house).

The lower sketch tells the same story but the saltbox here is the Andrews house in Bridgewater, Massachusetts. Compare the pitch of the roof with that of the Ogden house. The latter is close to the norm, but as the Andrews house indicates, there were—and are—no rules that a builder had to stick to the norm. Nor was there any rule that the pitch of the rear slope had to match that of the front slope. Usually it did, but sometimes the rear slope was slightly less steeply pitched in order to make for a wider first-floor room or to allow for more headroom in the attic. (And, as noted earlier, some rear slopes were bent upwards to achieve the same ends.)

Roofs on Cape Cod houses are more variable. Most are rather steep gable roofs (the average pitch is about 10 inches per horizontal foot). But a good number, especially in Connecticut, are gambrel

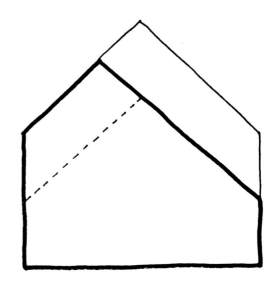

Ogden house, Fairfield, Conn.

roofs, used to provide better headroom in the attic. (A handful of saltboxes also have a gambrel roof in front). Neither kind of roof was broken by dormer windows in bygone days, but many old houses have since acquired dormers to improve headroom, light and ventilation, and almost all modern Capes now have them.

In these respects, Cape roofs were just like the roofs of conventional two-story Colonials. However, a few of the Capes built on Cape Cod boasted a unique feature: their gable roofs were bowed. Oftentimes the bow is so slight that it is hardly noticeable. Occasionally it is pronounced. On the Jabez Wilder house in Hingham, Massachusetts (Page 12), the roof is curved so much that the house is known locally as the Rainbow house. (For more pictures of this wonderful dwelling, see *The Cape Cod House*.)

There are several theories about why the roofs were bowed. The most prevalent seems to be that early houses on Cape Cod were built by shipwrights who simply enjoyed shaping roofs as they did the hulls of ships. Another theory is that home owners bowed their roofs to get a little more headroom underneath. A third idea is that bowing gave a roof better resistance to compression, thus strengthening it against the elements. Whatever the truth, the fact is that the bowed roof was not an American invention: The English had the idea first.

Both the saltbox and then, years later, the Cape passed out of popular favor because architectural styles and fancies had changed. Then in the early 1900s interest in Colonial architecture revived and a good many conventional two-story homes of Colonial and very similar Georgian design were built. Capes and saltboxes, however, did not arouse the same enthusiasm. It was not until after the depression began in 1932 that the Cape again took hold. One man was mainly responsible. He was Royal Barry Wills, a Boston architect. Wills loved Colonial homes and had a rare facility for designing them. He designed a great many two-story Colonials and a number of saltboxes, but the Cape Cod house was—at least in the public mind—his specialty.

Wills saw in the Cape the ideal answer for people with little money who wanted a new home adapted to the current way of living. He not only designed and supervised construction of Capes throughout New England but also publicized them

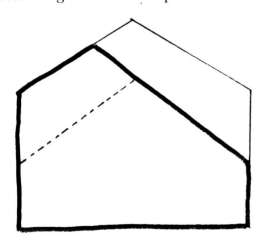

Andrews house, Bridgewater, Mass.

nationally in newspapers, magazines, books and through the publication of house plans. However, his message was not fully accepted until after World War II. Then the Cape Cod house quickly became the most popular home design the world has ever known. It was built by the hundreds of thousands from coast to coast.

Despite the fact that several of Wills' books also featured saltboxes, they were never as popular as Capes. Perhaps they looked too big to many people (for some reason they do tend to look considerably larger than they actually are). Perhaps people outside New England thought them odd-looking even though the houses have been and are built almost everywhere. Perhaps builders and developers, who have an acute, ingrained follow-the-leader, don't-upset-the-applecart complex, were simply scared to try them. Whatever the reason, new saltboxes were not built. But all that changed just a couple of years ago, probably in part because of the renewed interest in historic buildings generated by such organizations as the National Trust for Historic Preservation, the Society for the Preservation of New England Antiquities, Colonial Williamsburg, the Colonial Dames and thousands of community historical societies and historic district commissions.

Would you like to live in a saltbox or Cape? There are several ways to satisfy your desire.

1. You can buy a true antique house and fix it up as necessary. Depending on how much the house has already been remodeled, fixing may involve anything from simple painting, weatherstripping and installation of a few more electrical outlets to adding bathrooms, installing a heating and cooling system and building a large wing. You may even have to tear off all kinds of additions and excrescences before you start restoring the basic

structure. None of this is particularly easy; remodeling is almost always more difficult and expensive than new construction. But it is fun. And one of the prime advantages of restoring a fine old house is that our forefathers seemed to have built a great deal better and more sturdily than the builders do today, and they seemed to have had a better sense of design; therefore, you end up with a house that is generally better than the modern builder's effort.

2. You can buy an antique house, take it apart piece by piece, number the parts and move them to another location where you reconstruct the house—making the appropriate modern changes as you do so—on a better lot in a more desirable area. This, alas, is a truly costly operation even though you may be able to buy the old house for a song—or actually get it for nothing because, say, the highway department has marked it for extinction. But—this is the main plus of the approach—the house has all the advantages of antiquity in addition to all the advantages of the present. Because you tear the house apart and then re-assemble it, you can correct all its flaws—the drafty gaps around windows, the bulges in walls, the sags in floors, etc. The house is as sound and tight and lovely as it was when built in the 17th or 18th century, and it is still an antique but with modern conveniences. It is generally a better house than you would get by Method 1—restoring a house without dismantling it.

There are a few building firms that are in the business of salvaging and rebuilding houses in this way on a speculative basis. One that I have known for a long time is owned by Harry "Skip" Broom, a young man who has restored so many houses that he has become one of the country's experts. Currently, he is acquiring fine old houses from here and there around New England, dismantling them and rebuilding them in a wooded

Jabez Wilder house, Hingham, Mass.

valley in Lyme, Connecticut. The saltbox on Page 42 is one of these. It will probably cost quite a bit, but the person who buys it will have none of the headaches that are inevitably involved in the reconstruction of old buildings since Skip is doing all the work.

A similar company named Sunderland Period Homes, Inc. in South Windsor, Connecticut rebuilds older houses up and down the Connecticut River Valley. A couple of its saltboxes are also illustrated.

3. You can buy a brand new Cape or saltbox from a speculative builder. The pluses and minuses of this approach are well known because they are not restricted to just two styles of house: The initial cost of the house will probably be less than if you built the house yourself. But in the long run you may have considerable unhappiness because the quality of developer-built houses seems not to be very high. Furthermore, in an effort to cut his costs and in the belief that he is a good designer, the developer may have planned the house himself or had a hack architect do it; and the resulting house will not be so attractive and convenient in layout as a saltbox or Cape should be.

4. You can buy a plan from a plan service or copy it from a magazine or book; perhaps have it adapted to your own special requirements by a local

architect; and have it custom-made by a contractor of your choice. Several of the houses illustrated in the following pages were built in this way. It is a good way to hold down costs to some extent. But to achieve a very well designed Cape or saltbox depends on the skill and understanding of the person who designed the house in the first place, and of the person who adapts it for you—and here you run a chance of being gravely disappointed. Plan-service houses rarely turn out as beautifully as they look on the printed page. Houses featured in books and on editorial pages of national magazines are considerably better; but unless you pay the architects who created them to adapt them for you, you are at the mercy of a local designer to do the job.

5. You can perhaps find a builder of prefabricated houses that offers a good looking saltbox or Cape. However, the only company I know of that specializes in Cape Cod houses (not saltboxes) is Bow House, Inc., of Bolton, Massachusetts. This is an unusual firm that can provide plans for Capes, supply an architect to adapt the plans to your needs and sell a "package" consisting of just about everything that goes into its houses, including the curved rafters for the bowed roofs that are the trademark of the company, windows, doors, moldings, etc., but excluding basic materials such as framing members, masonry materials and kitchen cabinets. Actual construction of the house is done by a local contractor you choose under the direction of the company. A couple of Bow Houses are shown on Pages 130-131.

6. You can have a house designed to your special order by an architect who has a "feel" for Colonial homes and built to your order by a local contractor that you trust. Unless you insist on living in an honest-to-goodness historic house, this is the best way to acquire a saltbox or Cape that is excellent in every respect— appearance, livability and structural

quality—and not too terribly expensive. But I emphasize the need for employing an architect like Royal Barry Wills—a man who really loves saltboxes and Capes and knows how to develop designs that do justice to the Colonial style while satisfying your own 20th century living requirements.

That is a bigger order than you may think. For one thing, while there are many excellent architects, only a few of them are capable of designing good Colonial homes. For another thing, you must have a good understanding and appreciation of Colonial homes—specifically saltboxes and Capes—in order for you to pick the right architect and steer him in the right direction. That is why roughly half of this book is devoted to houses that were built long ago—so that you will know what they used to be like and how they have developed.

The saltbox or Cape that you build need not be a faithful replica of an old one. If you are going to live in the 20th and 21st centuries, it cannot be. Perhaps it can look exactly like an old house on the outside. Some brand new houses do. But the plan must be changed to encompass bathrooms, a modern kitchen and laundry, an up-to-date heating and perhaps air conditioning system, and so on. This usually, but not always, necessitates changes in the appearance of the house.

Such changes, if well planned and executed, do not spoil the house. What you must remember is that Cape Cod houses have already undergone many changes since they came into being in the 17th century. (Saltboxes have undergone fewer, less drastic changes.) Some of the most obvious changes that occurred in Capes are the following:

In the earliest houses the first-floor ceilings were only six-and-a-half to seven feet high and the heads of the windows and doors almost bumped against the eaves. But as time went by, ceiling height was raised and the exterior walls were stretched upward, so the space above windows and doors increased.

Earliest houses were devoid of ornamentation. But not for long. The trim around doors and windows was elaborated; cornices acquired dentils; bolection moldings framed fireplaces; summer beams that once proudly displayed adze marks were smoothed and carved; and so on. The simple Colonial style in which Capes had first been built was succeeded by the rich Georgian style, then by the more subtle and delicate Federal style, and finally—just before people lost interest in building Capes—by the Greek Revival style.

Windows that projected slightly from exterior walls and had heavy muntins gave way to windows that were flat in the walls and had slender Federal-style muntins.

Window placement in the gable ends became less eccentric. Dormers were added to roofs.

When heating stoves supplanted fireplaces, the great chimneys were reduced drastically in size. Even before this happened, some home builders deserted the center-chimney plan in favor of the center-hall plan. In this, a hall running from the front door to the back of the house was flanked on either side by two essentially square rooms, and there were two widely spaced chimneys each serving two or more fireplaces.

Still more changes were made after Royal Barry Wills revived the Cape. Although Wills was always faithful to the center chimney, which on his houses was larger than it had ever been before, other architects placed their chimneys wherever the plans required. There was usually only one chimney per house and it might be located at either end of the building or off-center between ends, and it might also be well in front of or behind the ridge instead of squarely on it. In fact, if a house has electric heat today,

chimney and fireplaces are sometimes eliminated entirely.

Windows have been enlarged; picture windows are common.

Almost all houses now start life with dormers. There are attractive gable dormers in front; but to provide maximum headroom on the second floor, big, homely shed dormers are commonly used in back.

Closets, which were virtually unknown in our ancestors' homes, are everywhere.

Stairs are straighter and less steep.

Kitchens are even bigger than in Colonial days. This was not always true, however. Royal Barry Wills' early kitchens were tiny because kitchen appliances were limited to a range and refrigerator and anyone who could afford to build a new Cape had a maid to replace the housewife as chief cook and bottle washer. (Poor maid—but at least she had her own bedroom and bath.) Furthermore, the washing and ironing were either sent out or done in the basement. But today, of course, the kitchen with its many appliances is the gathering place for the whole family as well as the housewife, so it must be enormous. And a laundry is essential.

Finally, the Cape has increased dramatically in size. Two hundred and fifty years ago the average full Cape measured out to roughly 1600 square feet (counting both floors). In the 1930s many houses were no bigger. Many, like the half and three-quarter Capes before them, were much smaller. On the other hand, quite a few were born with wings that doubled or tripled their size.

Today Cape Cod houses are, by and large, bigger than they have ever been. When I asked Richard Wills, who is now head of his father's old firm, to direct me to some of his newest houses, he remarked: "But you may not recognize many of them because they stretch for a hundred feet and more."

It is a fact: If you are going to build a

Cape for a family of four or five, with a family room as well as a living room, a bathroom for every bedroom, an attached garage for two or three automobiles, plus space for a riding mower, a couple of RVs, perhaps a boat and all the other paraphernalia Americans accumulate today, you will probably need at least a half acre to accommodate it. And because the cost of land is soaring, the once very economical Cape Cod house is no longer the bargain it used to be.

Here, perhaps, is another reason why the saltbox is suddenly being built again. Because it is a two-story house, it provides as much, or more, living space on a smaller lot as a one or one-and-a-half-story house of comparable size. In addition, two-story houses are somewhat cheaper to build than those of smaller stature.

Obviously, these are not new advantages. So why has the saltbox lagged in popularity behind the Cape and conventional two-story Colonial home? I can speculate on answers but have not found firm support for any of them. However, because the saltbox has lagged, it has not undergone the numerous changes that the Cape has experienced.

To the passerby, many of the saltboxes that are being built right now look almost exactly like those built in the 17th and 18th centuries. One minor difference is in the increased size of the windows. The sole major difference, which is noticeable only if you walk around behind a house, is that, whereas the rear slope of the original house was a huge unbroken catslide, that of new houses sprouts a variety of dormers, roof windows and/or skylights. This is not an esthetic improvement but it does add greatly to the usable living space on the second floor and perhaps in the attic under the roof ridge.

Inside, of course, the modern saltbox boasts all the conveniences and livability we expect of our homes. Its one drawback, according to some owners, is that even with larger windows it is somewhat darker than they like.

But major changes in the saltbox may be coming. Indeed, some have already been started. Along with the traditional saltboxes that are being put up today you will see an almost equal number of very untraditional design. Many, in fact, are so far out that the name saltbox just barely applies. "Houses with catslide roofs" is more appropriate. A number are pictured on the following pages. From the design standpoint, none of them is very successful. They lack the quiet, sturdy simplicity of the traditional saltbox. For this they substitute only the appeal of something new, something different—of change. But we should not condemn them just because they have so far failed to change gracefully. If and when good architects turn their hands to the task, a new Modern saltbox should establish a place for itself in America alongside the traditional saltbox and its old companion, the Cape.

Old Saltboxes

The George Hubbard house, 1638, is the oldest in Wethersfield, Conn. It has gone through many changes. It started as a two-room (one up, one down) house, acquired two more rooms on the right side, then the older section acquired a lean-to; and this later acquired a wing. At some point, the fireplace and chimney were removed, but these will be restored. The small windows throughout have diamond panes.

Guilford, Conn., and Ipswich, Mass., seem to have had a special love for saltboxes. Beautiful examples abound in both. The Caleb Stone house, 1748, is one of the loveliest in Guilford. The front roof is very steep. The long catslide roof breaks sharply upward near ground level.

When Lt. William Bushnell built his home in Old Saybrook, Conn., in 1680, it had just two rooms. Over the years it was enlarged into a saltbox, and then the saltbox was enlarged by an assortment of additions to the back of the house (see picture opposite). The latter do not add to the beauty of the house when seen from the rear. But thanks to the love and handwork of the owners, the house is a gem. Above is the living room (yes, the fireplace wall is buckled) and its corner cupboard. The old keeping room is below.

The dining room of the Bushnell house is splendidly paneled; the massive oak framing pieces help to explain why this and other ancient houses have survived so long. Note how the corner post is shaped to support the chimney girt. The corners of the summer beam are chamfered. The two main bedrooms on the second floor are pictured on the facing page. Both have small fireplaces.

The stairs in the Bushnell house are unique. The original stairs (left) in the entry opposite the front door form a tight U. Forty years ago, when two little bedrooms were built at either end of the attic under the roof ridge, the ceiling of the second-story hall was torn out and T-shaped "good morning" stairs (upper left and right) were built to reach them. Below is the small bedroom created in the second-story attic directly behind the chimney by building a big central shed dormer into the catslide roof.

The Hyland house, built in 1660, is one of the best
saltboxes in Guilford, Conn. As first built, the
house had overhangs on the front and both sides.
When the rear roof was extended downward in a
catslide, the side overhangs were not continued.

The Samuel Lee house in Guilford, Conn., dates from 1750; the Hoxie house (opposite page, top and right) from 1675. It is in Sandwich, Mass., and is much simpler, almost rustic, with the plainest kind of plank doors and leaded windows. In earliest Colonial times, people tried to face their homes south to catch as much of the sun's warmth as possible. But the Hoxie windows did not do the job well because they are so small. At immediate right is a large saltbox in Old Lyme, Conn. But in the 1800s, when the house was occupied by the seventh Chief Justice of the U.S., it was not a saltbox and faced the street rather than sitting parallel to it.

This beautifully maintained house in Clinton, Conn., was built in 1750. When I photographed it, the owners had just put it on the market because they felt it was too big for them; and as old saltboxes go, it is a bit larger than most. Its appearance, however, is illusory. Most saltboxes tend to look bigger than they really are.

The Bush-Holley house in CosCob, Conn., is famous because many noted artists and writers of the late 19th century, including Childe Hassam, Robert Frost and Willa Cather, lived there. But it is also of considerable architectural interest. It was built circa 1685, and acquired wings to the side and back much later. The double gallery facing CosCob Harbor is a late addition, too, but a very logical and splendid one that is worth copying.

Courtesy of "Southern Living"

The South has saltboxes —not many, but some. This is the Solomon Lick house, built in 1822. It is one of the many dwellings in the restored 18th century town of Old Salem in Winston-Salem, N.C. The break in the catslide roof is much closer to the ridge pole than it is in most saltboxes.

The Dudley House (c.1675) faces the Post Road in the center of Madison, Conn. The big shed dormer is less unsightly than most; it adds greatly to the usefulness of the attic created on the second floor under the catslide roof. Window treatment on the two sides of the house differs slightly.

The Jonathan Murray house in Madison, Conn., (below) is of the same general size and stature as the Winston-Salem house on Page 28. The extremely shallow overhang on the front and sides was very popular in Connecticut in early times.

Above and right is the famous Old Manse, in Concord, Mass. Built in 1769 or '70, it was the home of Ralph Waldo Emerson and Nathaniel Hawthorne. The house has a gambrel roof, but part of the rear slope was extended to make a catslide.

The Thomas Griswold house in Guilford, Conn., was built in 1774. The austerity of the house, perched well above the road, is alleviated only by the fine Georgian doorway. Inside, the house is partly Georgian, as in the living room, and partly simple Colonial. The kitchen (directly below) is almost crude. The huge fireplace, with two ovens built into the back, is flanked on the right by a semi-circular plank wall. You realize it is the back of a cupboard when you step into the dining room.

34

Here are two Rhode Island stone-enders. On the facing page is the Eleazer Arnold house, in Lincoln. It used to be a saltbox, as the picture of the end wall shows, then a sort of giant shed dormer was added, thus giving the house a normal gable roof. If the tree that mostly conceals the stone wall were cut down, you could see that when the house was first built in 1687 it was a much smaller saltbox—like the Clemence-Irons house above. The latter was built in Johnston, R.I., in 1680. Stone covers only about two-thirds of the chimney end of the house. The catslide roof is slightly curved. The bargeboards have interesting hooked ends. Windows in both stone-enders are tiny.

The Capt. Thomas Newson house, 1710, in Wethersfield, Conn., was not always a saltbox. The slight bend in the rear roof—at the same level as the eave in front—tells us that. A wing that stretches backward from the house was added even later. Unlike most double front doors, each panel of this one is wide enough so that when only one panel is open you can walk through without turning sideways. On the facing page is the Kingsnorth-Starr house in Guilford, Conn. Built in 1642, the house has been painstakingly restored in recent years. The shrubbery, unfortunately, conceals the lean-to, which was added around 1668. The fireplaces in the kitchen and old "hall" are enormous.

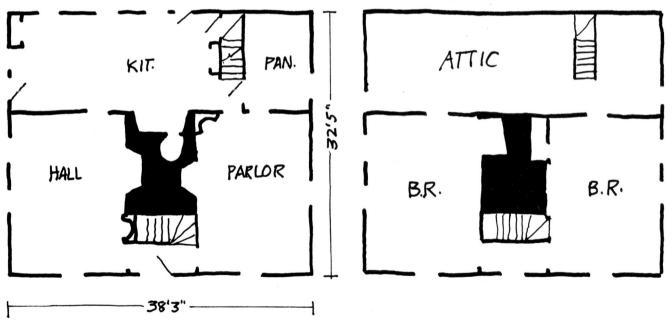

KIT.   PAN.

HALL   PARLOR

ATTIC

B.R.   B.R.

32'5"

38'3"

The Richard Gardner house in Nantucket (above) was built as a saltbox in 1690. When more space was needed, the owners made the odd decision to add a lean-to at the end of the house. I say this was odd because the lean-to does not enhance the beauty of the house and because the position of the chimney at the end of the house indicates that the first Mr. Gardner may have had an idea that he would some day extend the house under a gable roof to the right of the chimney. The catslide roof on the little Lyme, Conn., house at left was terminated long before it neared the ground. As a result, there is no wasted second-floor attic space under the roof.

If it were not for the historical marker at the corner of the David Osborne house in Fairfield, Conn., you might pass the house by as a modern copy of an old saltbox, for it has been wonderfully maintained. Because the house was built in 1784, it may have always had blinds. However, blinds were rare before about 1750.

The Job Lane house in Bedford, Mass. (above) is wondrous to behold. It was built in 1664 and looks it. The windows in the facade do not line up. The catslide roof is split more or less down the middle; one side is fairly steep, the other slopes gently backward for miles. Both sides undulate like the sea. The Thomas Lee house (facing page) started life in South Lyme, Conn., in 1660 and was built in several stages. In the process it is thought to have been, in effect, turned completely around. That is, the front became what is now the back, and the back became what is now the front. It was during this metamorphosis in about 1713 that it became a saltbox. The cramped entry, typical of the period, is at right.

This house, which was recently moved to Lyme, Conn., and is being reconstructed by builder/developer Harry Broom, was obviously far from finished when I photographed it. It will, however, be an exceptionally handsome saltbox. It was built in Avon, Conn., in the mid-18th century. Broom moved it from there and is adding a wing on the back. This will incorporate the front entry, master suite, part of the family room, and in the basement under the bedroom, a recreation room. Note the beaded siding and how the windows project from the walls.

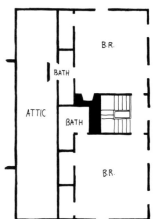

The saltbox at Hale Farm in Richfield, Ohio, was built about 1830. It is a small house with lie-on-the-stomach windows in the front wall of the upstairs bedrooms, which means there is less than the usual headroom at the front of the bedrooms. Because the house was built about the time that the Greek Revival style began to flourish, the doorway and living room fireplace are of simplified Greek Revival design.

The Hale Farm house and the Cape Cod house on Page 112 are among the very few old Colonial-style dwellings in northern Ohio, which originally was called the Western Reserve. This vast territory had belonged to Connecticut before the Reserve was created, and it was settled largely by people from that state and Massachusetts. Consequently, the area might be expected to abound today in old Colonial homes. But it does not, probably because the settlers were so busy establishing farms that their first homes were not much better than shacks. When they finally got around to putting up permanent homes, the Federal and—within a few years—the Greek Revival styles had taken hold throughout the nation, so almost all early Western Reserve houses were built in those styles.

The Guilford, Conn., house at left is charming despite the modern smokestack. The original house was very narrow; then the lean-to was added and after that the rear wing. Below, left is the Jonathan Fiske house in Concord, Mass. When it was first built in 1724 it was not anywhere near as long as it is now. On this page is the Josiah Dennis house, 1736, in Dennis, Mass. Like most houses on Cape Cod it is shingled (though saltboxes in New England were usually clapboarded). The left front windows on the second floor do not align with those to the right, indicating that the house was at first only half as long as it is today.

All the houses here are in Ipswich, Mass., and all have a Beverly jog. This is a small saw-tooth-shaped structure adjoining the rear corner of a house on either side. It got its name from the fact that it was evidently first used in Beverly, Mass., very close to Ipswich. It did not serve any set purpose, just simply added a little floor space to a house. At far left is the Glazier-Sweet house, 1725. The 1690 Caldwell house (above) has Beverly jogs at both ends. The plank door is barely 6 feet tall.

At right is the ancient Acadian house in Guilford, Conn. Originally, the catslide roof swept straight down almost into the ground, which slopes upward behind the house. Then the roof was given its present bend to improve headroom on both the first and second floors. Except for the new bath, the plan, drawn in 1936, shows the house more or less as it was when built, but the architect who drew it was not sure what the purpose was of each of the first-floor rooms. Both fireplaces contain ovens. On this page is the Cooper-Frost-Austin house, 1689, in Cambridge, Mass. Skylights were added to improve the old attic spaces. Pilastered chimney tops were quite common on early houses.

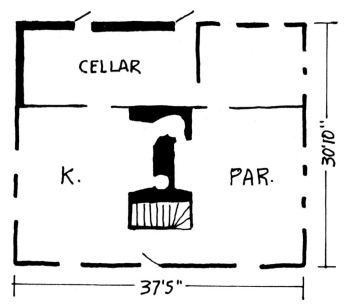

CELLAR

K. PAR.

37'5"

30'10"

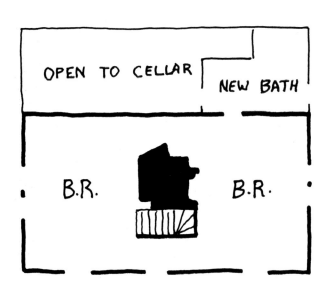

OPEN TO CELLAR

NEW BATH

B.R. B.R.

If you want to see almost exactly what an early 18th century saltbox was like, the Stanley Whitman house (this page) is one of the very best to visit. It was built close to 1707 and was painstakingly restored in 1988. It is in Farmington, Conn. The overhang is adorned with drops like that at left.

The gambrel roof of the Babcock-Smith house in Westerly, R.I., was extended downward at the rear to make a very spacious saltbox. The doorway opening into the vestibule is crowned by a handsome scroll pediment. The house was built in 1732.

The Jonathan Bronson house had only two rooms when it was built circa 1680 in Brookfield, Conn. It was added onto repeatedly over the years after that. The roof of the first addition—two more rooms on the other side of the chimney—did not line up with the original roof. A door was cut into the outside wall on the right end of the house and a covered stoop was built around it. A wing sprouted from the far end in 1820. By the 1980s the house did not look like much of a place but the basic lines were good and the interiors were excellent. So Sunderland Period Homes of South Windsor, Conn., bought the structure, destroyed the 1820 wing, dismantled the rest, and moved it to the Connecticut River Valley where they rebuilt it. Some of the results of the firm's work are shown here. An ugly duckling has been transformed into a swan. Everything in sound condition, such as the doors, the beautiful paneling and the sturdy oak timbers, was saved and reused. Whatever new materials were needed in place of the old or for installation in new rooms, such as the kitchen and bathrooms, were turned out in the builder's millwork shop. Unfortunately, most masonry materials had to be replaced entirely, but use and time will soon discolor the new materials so they no longer stand out as they do here.

The Parson Ashley house in Deerfield, Mass., has a saltbox roof very similar to that of the Babcock-Smith house on Page 51. The only slight difference is that the upper slopes of the Ashley roof are a bit steeper. But this is of minor note. What makes the Ashley house famous is its scroll-pediment doorway. Few doorways in the U.S. are as magnificent. A small pineapple, the old symbol of hospitality, is centered between the scrolls and the entire surround is elaborately carved. The door itself is also unusually handsome. The house had a checkered life. It was constructed in 1730, was later moved and used as a tobacco barn. Three-quarters of a century after that, it was moved back to Deerfield and lovingly rebuilt.

The saltboxes on these pages are a study in contrasts. The old house, in Madison, Conn., at the top of the facing page is pretty much a standard saltbox. The only slight difference is that the catslide roof, instead of ending at the foot of the steep slope, makes a rather sharp bend and continues outward and downward. The shed dormer was, of course, added long after the house was built. The house on this page is much older. It is the Joshua Hempsted house, 1678, in New London, Conn. It was enlarged several times. During one of these changes the rear roof was lengthened to form a gentle catslide. This is best seen in the closeup picture. The house at right, bottom, is the Jehiel Goodrich house in South Glastonbury, Conn. It looks like an undistinguished Contemporary house but actually dates to 1743. It, too, has undergone changes. In one of them the catslide roof was extended outward to protect a screened porch.

This house in central Connecticut was built by
Jacob Strong in 1698 and has grown from one room
into a saltbox with a two-story gable-roofed wing in
the rear. It has deep overhangs at both ends and
three exterior doors framed by beautiful matching
pediments and handsome pilasters. The first-floor
windows on the front and left side also have

pediments. In the parlor (above) the large over-
mantel panel is surrounded by a bolection molding.
An unusual wide, seven-panel exterior door swings
into the room; when open, it does not hang parallel
with the jambs because the exterior wall is not
plumb. The house was restored by Sunderland
Period Homes.

From the road, Whitehall, in Newport, R.I., is a handsome Georgian dwelling with a hip roof. Viewing it from the sides, you find it has a lean-to addition in back. This is not a pretty thing, but it makes the house a saltbox, which is why I show it. Whitehall began life as a much smaller house; took its present form after it was purchased by Dean George Berkeley following his arrival in America in 1729. Another peculiarity of the house is the doorway: the left panel has a wall behind it and does not open. On the opposite page is a splendid saltbox in Fairfield, Conn. It was built before the Revolutionary War and was once an inn.

New
Saltboxes

This splendid saltbox was built in Birmingham, Mich., only a couple of years ago. The owners soon discovered it was not big enough for them, so they added to the right side a narrow section. To avoid accentuating the length of the house, the addition was set back slightly and the front roof slope was lowered slightly, but the rear slope is a continuation of the original catslide. The attached garage is a saltbox facing in the opposite direction. The wainscoted living room to the left of the front door is shown on this page.

The family room (above), dining room and front hall of the Birmingham saltbox are illustrated here. The house opposite is in Newton Center, Mass. Designed by Royal Barry Wills, it was built in the early 50s. The front overhang is adorned by four drops much like those on the Whitman house on Page 50.

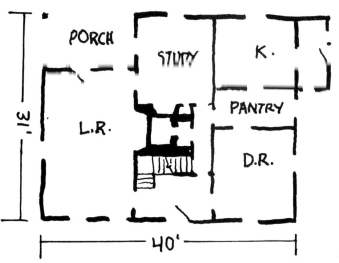

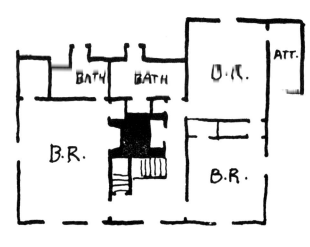

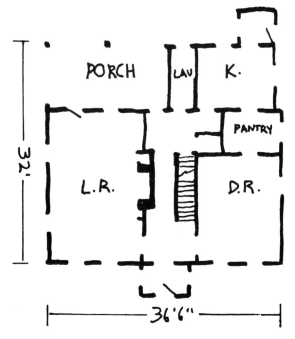

PORCH   LAV   K.

PANTRY

L.R.   D.R.

32'

36'6"

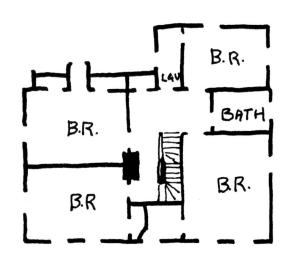

B.R.

LAV

BATH

B.R.

B.R.

B.R.

The saltbox at left is deceptively big. This is mainly attributable to its elevated position above the street, very steep roof and huge chimney. It was designed by Royal Barry Wills and like many of his saltboxes has a porch tucked in under the catslide roof and an overhang decorated with drops. The vestibule is a useful addition. The house is in Massachusetts. The saltbox at right and below is in Old Lyme, Conn. The doorway is a modern version of that on the Ashley house.

At left is a brand new saltbox put up on speculation in Plimpton, Mass. Since it is on a steep slope, it was logical to put the garage underneath, and except from this angle, this does not really spoil the looks of the house. In fact, the house fits its site very nicely because the catslide roof parallels the ground. The house below left, right and in the plans is in Melrose, Mass. It was designed by Royal Barry Wills at a time when most families had just one automobile. This is garaged in the back of the house and the Beverly jog.

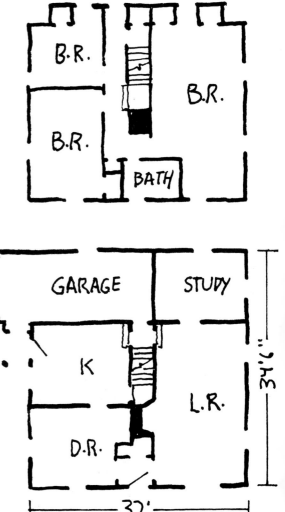

The house below, in Yarmouth, Mass., looks essentially like an antique saltbox, but it obviously is of very recent vintage. As in many early houses, the facade is clapboard, other sides shingled.

The two houses oppposite are in Old Lyme, Conn. The diagonal siding of the top one is unusual and effective. The front door of the bottom house is set in a deep recess that extends to the roof.

Katherine Hull

Both the Canterbury, Conn., house above and the Chester, Conn., house at right are new; and because they are on steep slopes they have balconies. The latter has a marvelous view to the right.

On the opposite page is a very unusual saltbox in New Seabury, Mass. The principal catslide is in the rear, but there is also one in front. The Old Lyme, Conn., house above has too many roofs and is less successful. Both houses make use of roof windows to bring light and air to rooms that are cramped in under the long roofs.

75

Three more unusual saltboxes: that at right, in Old
Lyme, Conn., the others in New Seabury, Mass.
Like most houses on Cape Cod, the latter two are
clad in cedar shingles that are allowed to weather
naturally. The Old Lyme house has vertical board
siding that accentuates its height.

In many of the ''new-style'' saltboxes, the catslide roof is on the front of the house, and the short roof is in back. That is the case in this tidy little house in Old Saybrook, Conn. The back of the house faces a pretty salt marsh, and there is a second-floor balcony from which the home owners can enjoy it. There is also a big deck at ground-floor level at the near end of the house.

Numerous houses are built like this one in Old Lyme, Conn., to look like a saltbox. But actually, the side walls of the shed dormer align or so nearly align with the walls below that the house is really a conventional two-story Colonial and might as well have been built that way. This might have looked better and would have probably saved some money by simplifying the framing

Opposite are new saltboxes in Sandwich, Mass. (top) and Old Lyme, Conn. They are of conventional design but differ in obvious ways and would require considerable study by a potential buyer choosing between them.

The saltbox in East Lyme, Conn., (above) is older than those opposite and benefits from more mature planting. It also benefits from the fact that it is more faithful to early saltbox design.

Some people have complained that saltboxes are a little too dark inside. This, of course, is primarily because the catslide roof blacks out the second story not only at the back of the house but also on the sides. Dormers, roof windows and skylights help to alleviate the first problem, but unless a shed dormer extends the whole length of the house, they help only partially, And the only way to light what used to be the second-story attic at the ends is to install tiny windows that admit little light. All this being so, the best way to compensate for the lack of light at the back of a saltbox is to install as many large windows as possible in the facade and on the sides. The designers of the two houses on these pages, however, failed to do this. And that means that the electric bills of the owners run higher than they might. But despite the shortage of windows, both houses are attractive. That above was built recently in Mashpee, Mass. That at right was built in Lexington, Mass., soon after World War II. The latter was designed by Royal Barry Wills and boasts several of his trademarks—a large chimney, a second-story overhang and a Beverly jog. The jog is quite a bit bigger than most.

A new saltbox in Templeton, Calif. More about it on the next pages.

Jim Ciskowski

84

We are accustomed to seeing saltboxes in towns and suburbs, but as this California house shows, they are just as beautifully suited to open country. The house was adapted from a design by architect August Suglia. Its most unusual feature is the two-story family room above and at far left). The interior treatment of the entire house is plain and simple; and walls are painted off-white to serve as a background for the owners' antiques. The front door (far right) is recessed. The owners wish the chimney were masonry but strict California building codes prevented that.

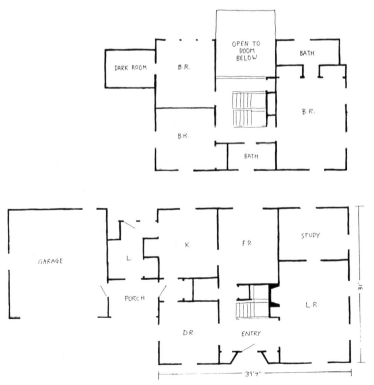

Old Capes

The house on the opposite page is one of a cluster of three perfect Cape Cod houses in East Dennis, Mass. It was built in 1795. One of its companions is on page 90. Below it is an older, simpler Cape, a long stone's throw from Long Island Sound in Clinton, Conn. On this page is a lovely Cape in Chester, Conn. It is dated 1780, but there is some evidence that it may be older. It was at one time a relay station and tavern on the stage coach line from New York to Boston.

Katherine Hull

This Cape is one of the East Dennis companions of
that on page 89. Despite its age and simplicity, it is an
unusually attractive house. This is in large part due to
the treatment of its door. This is lovely with its lou-
vered blinds, which also cover the fanlight, or without
(right). At the top of the facing page, a Cape in
Hampton, Conn., is much simpler—actually severe. It
was built in 1735. Below it is a younger Cape in
Killingworth, Conn. Its tiny chimney indicates that its
owners switched from fireplaces to a furnace for heat.
On the other hand, many homeowners have changed
heating systems without replacing their old chimneys.

90

Katherine Hull

The Watrous Beckwith House in Old Lyme, Conn., was built in 1789. It was a gambrel-roof Cape much as you see it (opposite, top). Later it sprouted a small wing. But, about 25 years ago, new owners tore off the back end of the wing and built a much bigger addition (bottom of page). The wing is a good modern replica of the old house, but no attempt was made to fool anyone about its age. On this page, the Chester, Conn., Cape (top) was built in 1787; the Killingworth, Conn., below it is about the same age but the basement rooms are a recent addition. The Killingworth Cape at the bottom is of Greek Revival design and is much younger.

When you add a wing to an antique house, do not try to match it exactly to the original design because that is a form of cheating and very costly to boot. Just try to emulate the spirit of the old structure so there is not a disturbing, sharp difference between new and old. In the Watrous Beckwith house, for example, the new bedroom (directly above) has a chair rail at the same height as that in an early bedroom (top), but it is not a slavish copy of the old rail. Similarly, the new stairs (lower picture) have the same "feel" as the old stairs (top) but they are quite different in treatment. On the opposite page is the living room in the old part of the house. This has not been changed.

Brick has never been a popular home-building material in New England and in early times it was hardly used at all. But after about 1750 a fair number of brick houses were put up in areas where bricks were made. So there is no reason to doubt that the house on this page was built in Canterbury, Conn. in 1760—as a plaque on the wall claims. One thing supporting this date is the bricks that were made at about that time for connecting the walls with stone foundations, which projected several inches beyond the walls. These were specially contoured at the outer ends to overlap the foundations in order to keep water from creeping in through the joint. They can be seen at right.

Both this house in Norwich, Vt., and that on the facing page qualify as Capes despite their brick walls and double chimneys. The use of two well separated chimneys instead of one at the center of the house came in when home owners decided that houses would be improved by running a hall from the front door to the back of the house. Still later, after heating methods were improved, one of the two chimneys disappeared entirely; and today some houses with electric heat may not have any chimney at all. These developments have not enhanced the appearance of the Cape Cod house. Personally, I still favor Capes with big center chimneys. But all architectural styles change to some extent over time, and any style of house that is as old as the Cape is bound to have changed considerably.

The houses on these two pages are half Capes. The doorway is at one end of the house and two windows are at the other. The chimney is usually at the doorway end of the house but not always. The house at right is a 19th century structure in Sandwich, Mass. The two below are considerably older and stand side by side in Yarmouth, Mass. That on the facing page is in Rockport, Mass.

When the owners of half Capes decided they needed more space, they usually enlarged their houses by adding a matching structure to the end that incorporated the fireplace and chimney. Thus, half Capes became full Capes. But the owner of this Rockport house added on, bit by bit, off the right rear corner of the house. So as you pass the house from left to right, what at first looks like a tiny place (as shown at left) turns out to be pretty sizable (below).

Because they are fairly small and old, Cape Cod houses appear to have an unusual tendency to grow (often in several directions). Whether they grow more than other styles of houses is a moot point. But grow they certainly do as is shown by the Benjamin Everist house, 1736, in Chester, Conn. (above), and by the sprawling 1797 Cape in Hyannisport, Mass.(top right). Below, right is the David Bushnell house, 1678, in Westbrook, Conn. Bushnell built the world's first submarine, the Turtle.

In 1759 Jonathan Warner built this Cape in Hadlyme, Conn. Almost 40 years later he crossed the Connecticut River and built a gorgeous two-story Georgian. But even his simple Cape displays a fine facility for working in wood and for excellent design—attributes you would not expect when you walk past the house. The fireplace in what was originally the kitchen is a beauty. There is nothing elaborate about it; it is just beautiful wood nicely handled. The summer beam in the parlor is cased with carved wood. The corner cupboard is also in the parlor.

Cape Cod houses with catslide roofs are not unusual. One of the favorite designs has a squat gambrel roof in front and a long, gently sloped catslide in back. This may have been a practical arrangement, providing a lot of space under a roof of restricted size, but it is not very pretty. These two semi-saltbox Capes in Guilford are attractive. The David Parmelee's house, 1780, below, is especially so, thanks mainly to the sweep of the front roof slope. I do not know whether the deep overhang was meant to keep out the western sun in the afternoon or to shelter family and visitors waiting at the front door from rain and snow, but it does both. The smaller, three-quarter Cape at left dates to 1774. Since it was a narrower and lower house when built than the Parmelee house, the catslide over the lean-to addition had to be connected to the old roof at a sharp angle.

These three houses are in Mystic, Conn. All were built roughly 150 years after the Cape Cod house developed, so they have lost some of the identifying characteristics of early Capes. The John Fellows house (below) dates to 1826. It is raised a story off the ground because it is set on a hillside.

The house above, right is the Hezekiah Park house. Built in 1840 when the Greek Revival style was popular, it shows Greek Revival influence in the doorway, cornice treatment and corner boards. The George Eldredge house (below) is simpler because it was built in 1791. The big chimney that it probably had at the start was torn down and replaced by a small one serving several stoves.

Here are two very simple Capes that exude irresistible charm. This is partly because they are sited above the road and overlook pretty valleys. But there is much more behind their beauty than that— though what it is I cannot say in a few words. The Ingham house, above, is in Old Saybrook, Conn. The other is in Lyme, Conn. Both were built in the 18th century.

The 18th century Cape in Westbrook, Conn., (above) is a little larger than most, and with its steep, overhanging roof provides more living space and more windows on the second floor than most Capes. The Chapman-Hall house in Damariscotta, Me. (below), was built in 1755. The eaves and rakes are trimmed back as far as they can be. Presumably this was done in early Capes so that the roofs would better withstand the winds howling off the ocean.

The Guilford, Conn., Cape above is dated 1787,
although the house appears younger because it was
not until the 1800s that the roof was commonly lifted
so high above the windows and door. The slight
overhang in this location is also unusual. Overhangs
were generally used only on two-story facades and end
walls. As noted before, Connecticut overhangs were,
by and large, much shallower than those in Massachusetts.

Todd Acker

This is one of the few Capes in the Western Reserve section of Ohio. (See page 43 for comment on this). It was built in 1831 in the town of Hudson by Prof. Elizur Wright, a Connecticut native who taught at Western Reserve College, which was then located in Hudson. Even with its screen door in place, the fan-lighted, side-lighted entrance is handsome. On the facing page is an older gambrel-roof Cape with center chimney in Old Lyme, Conn. Over the years it has been greatly enlarged. The doorway in the tiny vestibule is out of the ordinary, very simple but very charming.

Chester, Conn., is for some reason a hotbed of Cape Cod houses, though they are widely scattered throughout the town. Below is the Capt. Joseph Bates house, which was only half of its present size when built around 1810. The original structure and addition are not quite the same size.

The two houses opposite are also in Chester. At top is a three-quarter Cape built by John Warner in 1799. The full Cape (bottom) was built after 1759 by Reuben Clark. It has been much enlarged by subsequent owners. The long post-and-beam addition to the right of the main body is the most recent. The fences and terraces at both ends of the house make it look enormous.

114

The two Capes on this page were built in the early 19th century. That at the top is in West Barnstable, Mass. The doorway and partial quoins are unusual. The house in Killingworth, Conn. (right) was influenced by the Greek Revival style of architecture. Note especially the wide, plain frieze adorned by three medallions at the ends and center. The houses on the opposite page look equally old but are not. The Lyme, Conn., house (top) is 50 years old. That at the bottom is in Brewster on Cape Cod and is much younger.

116

Katherine Hull

New Capes

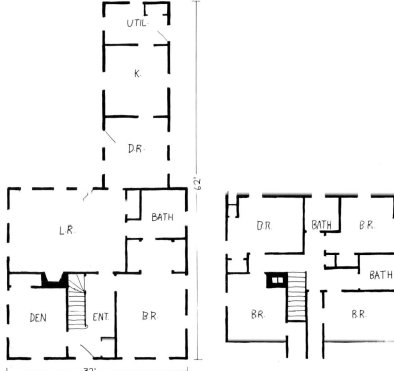

Capes with bowed roofs were quite common on Cape Cod in early times. Across the top of these pages is the only new custom-built house with bowed roof that I know of. It is in Hyannisport, Mass. It is a fine replica of the three-quarter Capes that were built in the late 1700s. But unlike early Capes, it started life with a long rear wing housing the dining room, kitchen and utility room. A garage was attached after the plans were drawn. Those shown are taken from plans copyrighted by Gaffney Architects, Inc. On the facing page is a more conventional but nonetheless attractive modern Cape in Old Lyme, Conn.

Stretched Cape Cod houses are as prevalent today as stretched limousines. Here are four examples: Above from Chester, Conn.; right from Barnstable, Mass; and both on the facing page from Sandwich, Mass. Despite the length of the dwellings, the central body in all cases is a half Cape.

This very attractive Cape in Birmingham, Mich., is almost as wide as it is long. Set on a typically narrow city lot, it has a detached garage. The plan is most unusual. The owners wanted a center-chimney Cape, but wanted a big central living room more, so the center chimney idea lost out. You are confronted by the dwelling's most surprising feature when you enter the front door: The entry is two stories high and behind it you can see all the way through the living room and across the bedroom hall upstairs.

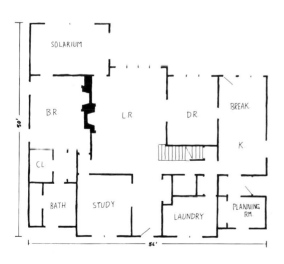

The Birmingham house featured on the preceding page is pictured at left. From the centrally located living room (top) you can enter the dining room, kitchen hall, library, master bedroom and solarium; and you can also climb the stairs to the second floor. This would seem to create a great deal of cross traffic through the living room, but actually most of it is funneled across the near end. And, anyway, the furniture is grouped around the fireplace so that anyone sitting there need not be seriously disturbed. The fireplaces and woodwork throughout the house were copied from antique models—but this is obviously a modern house, not an old one.

Above is a lovely little Cape in Old Greenwich, Conn. In an area of new and old houses of motley design—but some of very good design—it stands out like a beacon. I spied it through trees and buildings from the main road and knew I had to turn off on its lane to look at it more closely. I was not disappointed.

This house in Brewster, Mass., is simple, unpretentious and comfortable. The couple that built it just a few years ago like it, and that is the best test of all. Although the house has a center hall, the chimney is not too far off center on the roof. That is because the sole fireplace is set in the corner of the library—the owners' favorite room. Large roof windows light and air the second-floor rooms adequately. The plans shown are taken from plans copyrighted by Gaffney Architects, Inc.

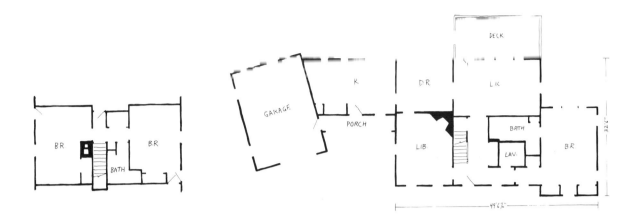

These three Massachusetts Capes were designed by Royal Barry Wills. The two small ones here are in a postwar Lexington development; the spreading house opposite is in Wellesley Hills. Wills designed about twelve houses in the development; the others, and there are many of them, were the work of the developer or hack architects. The Wills houses stand out like jewels.

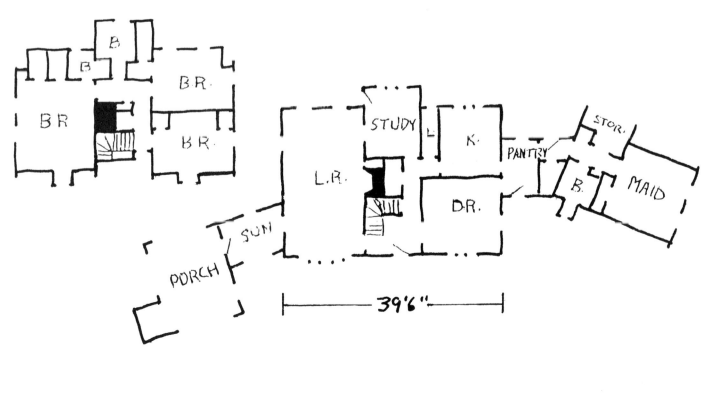

BR

B

B

BR

BR

BR

STUDY

L

K

STOR.

PANTRY

LR

DR

B

MAID

SUN

PORCH

39'6"

Above and at the top of the facing page is a half-size Bow House; at left is a three-quarter-size Bow House. The roofs are curved even more than on the old Jabez Wilder house on Page 12, but the houses are attractive and popular. These are in Connecticut; you will find similar houses all across the country. The plans are easily adapted to individual needs, and easily expanded, as these houses were.

The day will probably never come when the Cape Cod house is generally thought of as anything other than a traditional design more or less like the pleasing Sandwich, Mass., house below. But on the drawing board of a first-rate architect, the Cape can appear in very modern garb. Consider the long, low house, right, in New Seabury, Mass. It was designed by Royal Barry Wills. More on next pages.

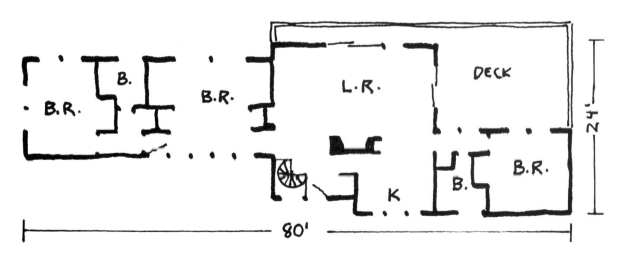

Lisanti, Inc.

New Seabury is a huge new residential development on the south shore of Cape Cod. When it was established several decades ago, Royal Barry Wills was asked to design one of the model houses for it. The ultra-modern Cape shown here and on the preceding page was the result. It may not exude the nostalgia of a Cape built along ancient lines, but it is extremely attractive and rather obviously a delight to live in.

Despite the appeal of Royal Barry Wills' New Seabury Cape, this is the kind of Cape that he was noted for throughout the United States. Wills himself, in one of his books, described Capes as follows: "A glimpse of a wide doorway, of white clapboards in the sun, of bittersweet in the garden—such are the houses of Cape Cod. They line the quiet, shady streets of the villages—as unpretentious as they are livable. Carping critics may poke fun at their rambler roses, picket fences and stately elms, but such things spell home to most of us." This little house spells home.

Although the emphasis today is more on big Cape Cod houses, small ones are still built in large numbers. This was particularly true several decades ago; it may become true again if construction costs keep soaring. In that case, we shall see more Capes like that on the opposite page. It is in Old Lyme, Conn.; the two here are both in Birmingham, Mich. They are all very pleasant. However, the one at right should be viewed only from the front (an obvious impossibility) because a homely addition—some sort of shed dormer—spoils the back of the house.

The New Seabury, Mass., house above is unusual because the entrance is not in the section at the right end but in the connector. The Cape (right) in Birmingham, Mich., is representative of the kinds of Cape most often built in the 1950s. The Old Saybrook, Conn., house across the page just misses being a dead-ringer for that on Page 144.

When the owners of the house below, in Old Lyme, Conn., were starting it, they were nice enough to say they had used my earlier book on Capes as a guide and inspiration. True or not, they built an attractive house that appears to fulfill the family's requirements without fuss and feathers.

The New Seabury, Mass., house at right is another attempt to make a Cape more modern in feeling. It succeeds quite well. The long, low, white Cape in Barnstable, Mass., acquired the wing at the left when the owners went into the antiques business. They kept the shop in good proportion to the house so that, if someone ever wanted to use the whole building as a dwelling, they could easily do so.

The owners of this
gambrel-roof Cape in
Old Saybrook, Conn.,
owned an almost
identical twin twenty-
odd years ago. They
liked the first house, a
Royal Barry Wills
design, so much that
they built it again on a
wooded site over-
looking the Con-
necticut River. Of
course they made a few
minor changes, which
included enlarging the
windows facing the
view to the rear of the
house. They also
enclosed the open
porch to make a sun-
room. More on the next
three pages.

The living room of the Old Saybrook house on the preceding pages is to the right of the small entry. It is large and bright, with two windows in front and two bay windows in the wall opposite the nicely detailed fireplace and French doors at the back. The dining room, pictured on Page 148, is behind the entry and staircase. It has a fireplace in one corner and a built-in cupboard in the opposite corner.

Dining room of the Old Saybrook house (top). The two pictures at right are of an office off the end of the dining room and two steps down. It is behind the kitchen, in the connecting link between the house proper and garage. Above is one of the bedrooms. All the rooms at the back of the house have big windows to bring in the view.

This Old Lyme, Conn., house is another modern version of a Cape. But actually, on examination, the modern look is attributable only to the long, narrow windows. The roof is very steep but not a great deal more so than on some old Capes.

Unfortunately, the only accurately descriptive word for the floor plan is "crazy." But the house was recently bought by a couple who are both architects and they are planning major changes that will straighten things out.

Here are two more Capes with unusually steep roofs. That below is in Brewster, Mass. It is a striking small house—a half house with a little wing at the chimney end and an even smaller wing connected to that. By this arrangement the owners have assured that the half house cannot be turned into a full Cape unless the wings are cut off and either moved or demolished—which is rather drastic treatment.

This steep-roofed three-quarter Cape is just off the King's Highway in Barnstable, Mass. To the passerby it looks like a more or less ordinary but attractive Cape on a flat lot. But because the ground falls away sharply, it is actually three stories high in the rear and looks over one of the many small, dark fresh-water ponds on Cape Cod. This makes the house a double delight.

The scene is southern California in the vicinity of Los Angeles. The Cape at left—not quite so small as it looks but small enough to be mostly hidden by trees and automobiles—is a bona fide Royal Barry Wills design. The other houses are typical of what Californians call Capes. At the bottom of the facing page is a tract house built after World War II. It measures only 800 square feet. The chimney is a fake; there is no fireplace. Above it is a bigger Cape with a real center chimney. On the Cape above, the roof is steeper but the chimney is off-center. One detail that is common in California Capes is the recessed doorway.

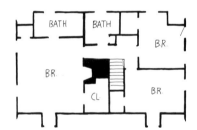

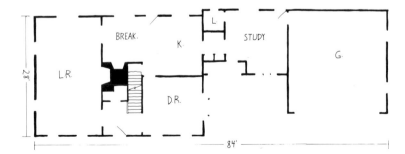

The owners of this Lyme, Conn., house saw sketches and plans of it first in a national magazine. They liked it, knew the name of the architect—Royal Barry Wills—, and bought a set of working drawings from the magazine. They asked their builder to make a few changes; the garage for instance, had to be brought forward so it would not slide down the hill behind the house into the Connecticut River. And then they built it and have lived in it happily for 20 years. The one big change they have made is to build a multi-level terrace overlooking the river. More on next pages.

At left is the living room of the Wills' house in Lyme. The fireplace is exactly as Wills designed it, but the multi-paned picture windows are the owners' idea. Below, left is the dining room with bay window facing a garden area between the house and the garage.

The study (above) is in the link connecting house and garage. Like the adjacent kitchen and breakfast area, it is paneled in knotty pine.

Above is the breakfast area at the living room end of the kitchen. At right: Looking from living room entrance through breakfast area and kitchen to the study beyond. The ceiling in this entire area is beamed.

Here are three Cape Cod houses of the type most frequently built today. You have seen hundreds like them, yet you cannot help being attracted by them. The house below is in Mashpee, Mass.; that at right, in Lyme, Conn.; that at bottom right, in Sandwich, Mass.

Two more delightful
but conventional
Capes. The only
unusual feature of
either one is the quoins
on the little red house
in Lexington, Mass.
The white house is in
Riverside, Conn.

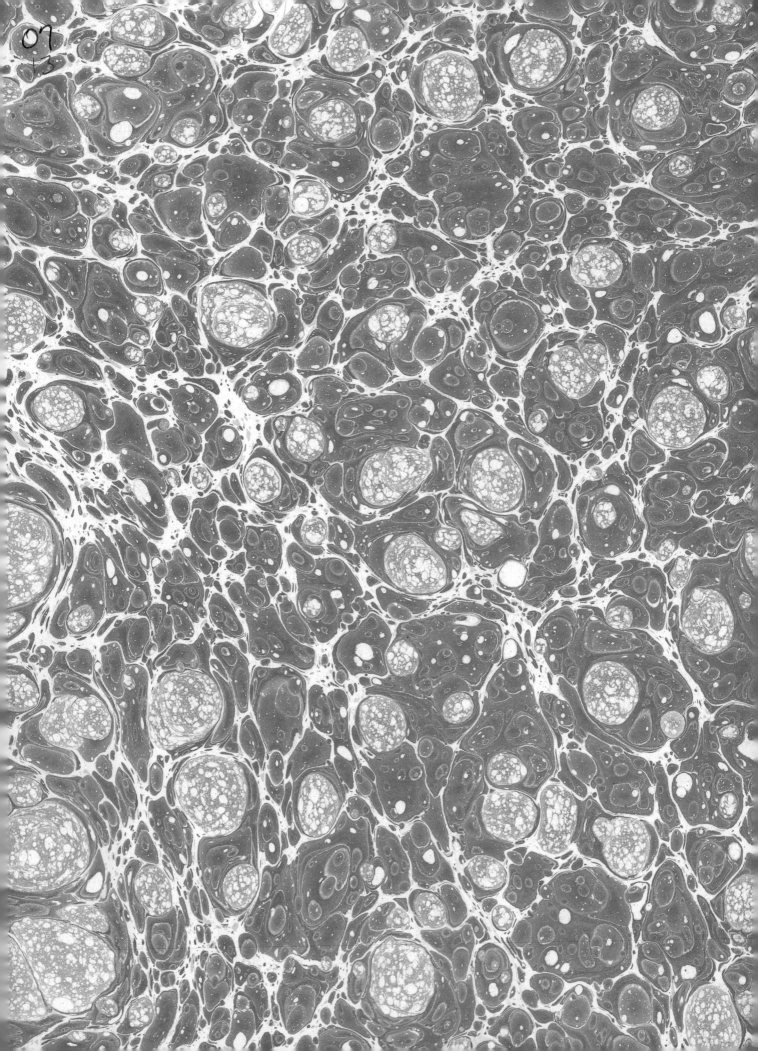